Forgive Me
If My Volume Offends You

Richard L. Toney

Copyright ©®2014, Richard L. Toney
Toney, Richard L.

FORGIVE ME IF MY VOLUME OFFENDS YOU
The Burning Heart Vol. 1

Published by
Life in Print Publishing
978-1-7356232-0-7

www.lifeinprint.org

All rights reserved under International Copyright Law. No part of this book may be reproduced or transmitted in any form or by any means, electronic or mechanical, including photocopying, recording, or by any information storage and retrieval system, without the written permission of the publisher.

Feb-04
Rev. 9-20

1. Inspiration – Christian Life 2. Faith – Poetry
3. Devotion – Christian Living

Dedication

The words and thoughts of this compilation are inspired by the great crowd of witnesses that keep me in the way when adversity tests me to fall back.
For such a company of people to be under one roof, one name, one family; I am truly blessed to be one and kin.

With all I am I thank you and thank God in praise for your health and strength.

About the Book

This collection is a beginning; an abridged look into the journey of making. From writer to writing I share this trip with you. The first step on a lengthy road with all the twists and turns afforded me. This record speaks volumes sometimes at a volume unexpected. However it is the first of what is hoped to be many breaks in the serious work of faith and enduring the details of living.

This collection represents both a bold statement of faith and a moment (moments) of levity. May you enjoy its message and know. I laughed and I cried recording these works so it is to be expected that anything could happen.

Cry with me. Laugh with me. Take some insight away from these pieces but overall enjoy yourself.

Contents

Dedication	5
About the Book	7
Contents	9
Soul and Matter	13
The Tune	15
Encounter at Faith Hall	17
The Light to Come	18
A Simple Song	19
The Light at Nearly Dawn	20
My Tithe	22
Perish the Thought	24
Even the Coolest Fall	26
The Storm is the Warning	28
Salvation	30
The Becoming	32
To Him My Song	34
The Night Season	37
The Revelation	39
Victory	40
Of Roads we Travel	41
The Collusion	42
The Darkness that Hides	44
Thy Brothers Been Tempted	46
The Seeds Were Sown	48
The Unseen Hand	50
Elevator Dreaming	52
Arise	54
Daydreaming	56
The Morning Prayer	57
Less of a Reflection of We	59
Unseen	61
My Fathers Voice	62
Things I Thought of When I wasn't Allowed to Sleep	64

The Mind's Ear	66
The Addict	68
My Cup to Drink	70
The Tyranny of Man's Love	72
The Truly Desperate	74
The Gift	76
The Point Advantage	78
Shake It Off	80
The Road Less Traveled	82
This Road is Dangerous	85
The Power in You	86

The Taste of Sour Milk — **89**

Fatal Rose	91
Too Hungry to Eat	92
The Fear	94
Children	96
Blood and Water	100
Low Rent Construction	102
Hunger Pains	104
Little Mountain Pass	106
A Song of Adoration	109
The Climb	110
A Prayer of Faith	112

Dear Brother - No More Am I Afraid — **115**

The Cure	117
The End of Vanity	118
An Impasse	120
The Weight of the World	122
Broken Bread	124
Conversations With Kin	126
With Respect to Woman	128
Remembering Loves	130
A Song of Beauty	132

The Exit Psalm — **135**

The Origin	137
Of Plain Existence	138
The Wailing Mirror	140

The Wailer	141
Beyond the Friendly Confines of Adoration	142
Remembering Jehosophat	144
Beyond	146
The Passage	148
Maturity	149
Awakening	150
To My Father In Heaven	153
A Simple Inference	159

Soul and Matter

Let me suggest for a moment
As we probe into the deeper well
The moment becoming a mellow haze
I share with you
I am…

Existing to serve -
With purpose defined
I strive to understand why
I am

I choose –
Who I love
Where to go
Which way to live
God shall I serve
I fall
I hurt
I am…

Defined by moments –
Success and trial
I, this man
A living well
Alive
I Am

Heart and mind and soul
Together
Aware of He
Standing with me
Calling from deep

Come to me brother;
There is water to drink

Forgive Me

The Tune
01

I wouldn't call myself a singer. I wouldn't even call myself a good vocalist but I do have a song to share. A few words that may give some insight into a life – the life that speaks volumes sometimes at volume's peak.

Please allow me this composition and I suspect you will find yourself in concert with me. Free!
To be who you are. To sing!
To sing, as I do, my praises to Him.

I pray my heart aloud. I dare be heard and speak with His voice.
The words - His. The music and tone.
I am the image! I am who I'm called to be! Most passionately pursuing this song which all the world will know. The life that he gives - in you is the light that shares, Hallelujah.

Forgive Me

Encounter at Faith Hall

Who am I, so many would ask when given a chance to speak?
I say it as they'd all before
I never desired to preach.

I wouldn't try to stand with man
Leading him in simple prayers.
At every turn
Giving them words like,
God said!
I am just - a man.

Neither would I dare prepare
Content to rest in quiet praise.
But then the moment, it comes for me
How much more to be afraid?

Looking back from lofty heights
Thinking this too great a stand?
I ask considering
What happens to me?
What happens to those, if I fail?

The Light to Come

The stories,
The promises,
The Hope for a view;
A wish they said would speak.
What I hear – Is it you?

Is it you?
Setting a mood
Creating a tone
No incense no myrrh
We all in here
In search of a truth
Listen they say.

I've squandered my youth.
Walking - apart,
Thinking within
Listening for him; for heavens reply
My God,
How do I understand?

My feelings - my eyes,
With logic confused,
I believe it possible,
They said we'd hear
From you, have I gone too far?

Am I gone so away to steal embrace
Yet here, I yearn…
They say He speaks
Yet will I hear,
When everything I've known has changed?

A Simple Song

There is a rhythm in the air
The music enveloping
Compelling me to sing
I lift my voice.

With sound, to men, I give these words
Love is life
God is love
Together in heart. A song we sing

The song I hear in blades of grass
The waving trees…
The birds and bear
I hear His gift
And I,
I am
His words.

The Light at Nearly Dawn

You say as you're seeking God
How can this be the way?
I wash - I plea
I yearn - I reach
Crying with despair
I desire the truth
Yet the pain remains.

Am I to tell the world then, I confess
I'm guilty.
I was enamored with sin.
So the world should know what I say to him?
Your son is fallen away.

Could it be a simple reveal?
I am as I've chosen to be.
Shamed by this man
Shamed before you
The world now knowing
The darkness has fled from me
Yet I am laid exposed.

Here with what's left of my youth
The dust didn't flee
It simply waited around and settles down.

Again I more bear the stain
Once more unclean I've settled in heap
I say it more fervently.

Am I really seeking God?

Could this be His way?

I Plea
I speak - as silence falls
There is nothing for me to hide
I've given death this word

I will live on.

My Tithe

I give myself to Him…
God, willfully
Because I fail willingly
I choose to give myself to Him
My tithe.

Given life and eternally debted with no way to pay,
I give what is given to me
My gift
My life.

A life less lived and more bound by questions
Can I serve him?
Can I be true to him alone?
Will I ever reach the purest love?
Is there more than an idea to be shown?

A definition beyond the mere
God so loved the world that he gave…

His only begotten son
He gave.

Eternity in life,
He gave.

For me,
For every man
A gift
Yet the world is still become bitter.

Hindered in His touch
The gift we would share

Richard L. Toney

God.
Father.
Creator.

We are but men
I am but man
Fallen and in need
I am finished,
My will is done
and so I give in to Him…

Perish the Thought

Everything in this world isn't meant for me - I concede this
Yet that doesn't mean I don't want it all
Wanting some hint of the forbidden
Another roving expedition unfurls in the night's underbelly
I wander…

Why is it these things intrigue me so
Why am I so amused?
Why, if I've confessed I'm reborn
I should be free
I should be cured
Yet, my desire refutes…

My soul sinking…
Could this be what I am?

Could it be hidden in me?
A secret desire I've never faced
A silent wantonness too long ignored
Are these a part of me
Is this why I have strayed

My mind yearning to be free, yet I hide
Denying the want
The wantonness –
Longing to be clean
While knowing and kneading, wallowing in poverty…
Neglecting the very gift which says to me
Eternity lies ahead

Truthfully - just over the rainbow
Left of the dream
Deny your instincts a moment I hear;

Richard L. Toney

I would not
I cannot
I'm content with being…

Even the Coolest Fall

It began earnestly
A natural desire to admire beauty
To experience every sense His of creation
To know, to taste
To eat, to be filled.
To quench the desire of man lest he return to the dust.
After all
We must feed
We must eat
Yet he;
Thinking he could - tries to resist
All too aware…
There's a poison going around

Passed around
Traveling with no feet
It's tempting to touch it
To pet it
Yet he hides a bitter reality
A biting truth
There's a poison going around

Behind such beautiful patterns
Beneath the intricate colors
There's a sinister nature
A fatal heed for any who ventures too close
Beware his temptation
There's a poison going on

Misleading many
Feigning weakness
Drawing the masses in search of love
In search of the beauty of life

Could it be so deadly
A tiny morsel
Lethal and cruel
There is this - poison going around

Fueled by lusts
Fueled by the hidden nature of these yearning to be free
Choosing instead to be bought and sold
Surrendered to the want
I must experience the beauty
I must…
Ignoring the truth
There's a poison going on
And I too it seems risk my life

The Storm is the Warning

There is a rain approaching
Lingering in the distance
Contained
Held away from the fields I've tended since birth
Pray, as I will,
The drought is still here
I still have needs
I thirst for this promised drink.

Fill me
Complete me
End my wither
Whether I'm meant to be or sent to end
I thirst
I hunger
I pray,
Yet the storm lingers still
I wonder is this all His world I'm here to see.

My salvation moments away
In a distance yet restrained…
Held back from me… am I, was I, ever worthy
I won't consider
I know
I must prepare for him.

Holding my stance, lest me and my cup are blown away
I won't consider the chance
I know this rain is meant for me
So here I stand.
Remain?
Slightly leaning
Withering

Becoming one with the dust which surrounds me
I take his hand as he whispers,
Soon your life is going to change.

Salvation

Let me break for a moment
   the tension I had spared myself in ignorance
I ignore my pain
I ignore your ability to bring chaos
I live
Unfazed by the arrogance of accepting
Christ Is… the Lord

You should know this
I should know this
The world is as it's always been
Free to choose whatever is meant to believe.

The work, I had spared my self
Ignoring what we have come to understand
Salvation is of the Lord.

Freedom
Peace
Survival
The things we indulge
Almost to the point of worship,
Praising the success of bringing one closer to him,
   while the message goes unheard
Salvation is of the Lord.

The fields, being ripe with fruit
   as the many discuss who owns the land
Freedom it seems too has a price
A price I soon must repay.

I pay this price though
   Willingly

The same cost as you
because times have gotten away from us.

We the scattered
As they divided,
   alone.
The world awaiting the voice of Him
The world awaits
I pray
How soon, My God - how long?

The Becoming

As long ago as yesterday
I prayed to Him my prayer being
This day the day I become a man
With view and vision of less than perfection
My inflections intensify
I will to be what I will become
I will to be the image of man.

Father
Servant
Son
Complete.
What does it mean?
With failed understanding
My view – my vision
They seem a success
I don't have it.
I must reach
I will to be the image of man.

Not necessarily what you think
But I will manage
What I must reach
I will to be successful
In keeping with the search for me to be
Complete.

I will to reach God?
Someday
Someway
My purpose a feeling less meant for explanation
Wherever He is
I will to be

I will to attain.

Wherever – I would discover
I must go
I know that His word - it means success
He breeds successful
And of such stock I'm made
In the day of my one way
I will to reach Him
I will meet success

The only word I pray is…
Lord what will you have me be?

To Him My Song

There is as day would dawn
A new song
A quiet psalm
The words myself I couldn't sing
My voice to me not strong enough
But warm is the touch of His amen.

Embraced as they say it
When hearing these words
Halle –
Lu – Yah
Halle
Lu
Yah
In my solemn song
I lift Him up.

My voice to sing
My hands to praise
Halle –
Lu – Yah
Halle
Lu
Yah

A chorus and harmony we all embrace
The Lamb is worthy
Of God is grace
Halle -
Lu – Yah
Halle
Lu
Yah.

Richard L. Toney

Forgive Me

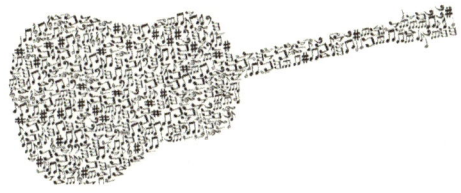

The Night Season
02

Waking in the heart of the night, a thought occurs to me, could these images be real? Are my thoughts, my eyes, deceiving me even as I recall the ordeal I share with you? I ponder and then now confess, I did sit silent while they chose to sin? Could Daniel, I wonder, find faith in this? Would Paul?

The darkness swallowing a life only I'd known. My heart growing disquiet as I remember the feeling of dying alone… Believing I too would be soon dead.

Surrendered to mortality, falling to the deceit, becoming what I despise the most, a man most suspect.
Faith, being long ago buried away, strength having times since failed and hope, a string seeming he'd torn from my grasp… I wonder… is this the way it's meant to end?

Seeing no sudden answer I begin pursuing him. Praying, crying, screaming relentlessly… is there some other way… Is there some hope to stymie my fate?

In silence I fall back into sleep. Going again into the dream,

seeing myself returned to the darkness, realizing then - there is something different with me…
A Hope - a prayer.
No longer am I crying alone.

The Revelation

There once was a dream
That lived the life of the dreamer
Flailing along…
Passing the time in the company of thinkers

Thinking…
One day… We will rise
One day… We will sing
One day…
We will be heard on the rooftop of sea floors
The world to be changed
The dream shall live
    And so too shall we…

Proclaimed,
    as they lay dying…
Wounded in their sleep
The King had returned
To find all had defied him

Victory

Every day I'm alive is a victory
The air I breathe
The sights I see
Are living proof to me there is more

More of a comfort but I can never rest
Would never because there are forces after me
Forces

Fighting a battle that never ends
A battle so fierce you have to extend until you are spent
Yet even then there is still no rest for your mind

For soon there will be more enemies
It would seem that these battles are merely testing me
No one is meant to win
Yet there is a loose reminder
The war was won before it began
It was won

I've got the victory

Of Roads we Travel

I had dreamed a dream
Although it seemed to me more a riddle
The times I knew I recognized
The others I would contemplate…
Why is this man so prone to darkness?
Why is it I see but shy away?

His hand outstretched offering peace
Yet there's no purchase for me
My eyes I turn
My back more stout
Why would I risk what's been gilded for me?

Could I or would I tend his wounds?
Should I lay my pack aside?
I wonder as the scene ensues
I live this dream
This time more real…
More pained
My eyes this time can't look away
It seems I have become the man

Wounded - disgusting – arrogant in need…
It seems there would be hope ahead
But reality brings a justice to me

I thought I had wakened - I slept
I thought I'd awakened - I lied
I AM NOT the wounded child
I cry…

Yet time will not concede
It seems -
Sometimes it's easier for men to look away

The Collusion

As darkness falls it all begins again
A night which never ends for me once more appears
I lie
Motionless.

Knowing of this impending trial
I face it tonight as with every night.
A break in the days when they said I'd be safe
Again he draws lying.

He's no friend of mine
His sorrow nothing more than a disguise
He lies
Once more my shadow moves in slowly,

The darkness becoming a veiled whisper
I long for the day this torment ends
Yet that day comes – it goes and comes to no end
His call beginning to sound more fervent
"Honey I'm going upstairs"
I retreat hoping tonight, dear father, the devil would not dare
Not tonight I cried
A lie to myself it seems…
The devil does not fear me

He knows I live my lie silently
Never to the world would I tell
Thinking…
Could it really be so bad?

I don't think
But, do I know
I tremble –

I think the darkness is gotten to my mind
The disease again prepared to have its follies
I feign asleep

Hoping…
If only I could dream
The demons dare not bother me if I were soundly sleep…
 Perhaps day then would not tarry
I imagine –
But then silly me…

My torment continues
Whether I wake or sleep
I am to be
I am to He
Chosen…
Hope is not running in
Damned if she would ever interfere
My heart becoming slightly more bitter…
Bring me your pain I scream.

Do as you will
This nightmare ends now
The door sounds…
kaboom!

My tormentor is fallen to the floor dead

The Darkness that Hides

How can I be party to such despisable things?
To witness without speaking the acts of a terrible man
Surely my heart could not lust for this
Surely my mind cannot imagine such horrible things
So why am I contorted by this ravenous beast?

A sheep, as gentle as I,
I would rather flee than continue to see
Yet I stand in the middle with this horrible man
Without shame
Without fear
I don't even look away
As it pains me to think…
The horrible things I've seen

Perhaps this is why I dream so despicably

Is it even possible for me to dream something more?
Something more serene, more peaceful in nature
I ask…
But then I reflect on all I've seen

Every innocent image - entertainment I protested
Every scream and splatter was only some well-rehearsed scene
So easily I laughed…

Get up stupid –
Run fool -
Hey dumb ass don't hide in the closet
It's funny…
They made a common mistake of life…
Don't look back too long

I wonder then… what does that say of me?

Am I really party to these despisable things
Deplorable imaginations -
Is it really so detestable to me
It seemed so innocent…

It was until it troubled me, now I wonder…

Why am I unafraid of death?
Why do I visualize such mean things?
Why am I - not disturbed at being disturbed?

Could it be?
I've already seen too much

Thy Brothers Been Tempted

A delicious basket of fruit I tried
One of each
I can't say why
But I chose to take a taste.

Just as well had been a mouthful
Call it curiosity
Call it fate
Whatever it suits
This day I made the mistake.
I bit the apple.

I didn't even resist.
At least not knowingly,
I ate
A sample I did willfully
Wanting to subsist
At least considering the fight
I resist… But slightly.

Perhaps if I'd stayed away
But then I had to have a bite
A small bite this day and
Suddenly I'm swayed
I've wandered into the garden where all eyes see.

Hoping no one is looking
All while knowing everyone is wide-awake.
Someone could have stopped me
Prevented my lapse of faith,
Instead…
They all sit and laugh.

Richard L. Toney

Smirking until they realize ...
We all shall share this fate

The Seeds Were Sown

He hid his face from me
His truth
A necessity I would not seek.
Dare I think to question he,
The man that I would call my friend?

A man who could see as me
I naive
Perhaps my fate holds the true answer

A question for which I've shown little concern
Why would I?
He thinks as me
We speak of things
Green perhaps,
but I know the limits of my right and wrong
Am I then so truly naïve?

I can see the death of night
I concede the alms of day
Should I fear the worth of he
A man to be believed my friend
He has never sent me wrong
Nor has he ever judged me

I believe - I can state…
My hope has never been denied with him

You say he lies…
But all have tried and made mistakes
Why then is it good to say
Watch that man

Richard L. Toney

He is no good
He has made many lose their way

The Unseen Hand

Delusion they call it,
To imagine there are forces unseen.
The media,
How do all those channels get to so many screens?
The wire, any wire, where everyone is listening.
Cell phones, internet; people talking but not saying a thing.
I believe in the good of the people but what good are the people
if they no longer believe.

What they see. What they hear. What is there?
Is it the air I breathe?
My asthma and allergies would argue.
Is it the water I drink?
As poisoned as ever but I don't question these things.

I don't
I do
Question who's who or what is real.
What is faith and what has faith become?

Some visionary instruction destined to lead
Some hidden potential yet to be captured
I ask
Is any of it true?
So truly complicated, Thank God...
I don't understand the answer, Thank God...
But why does the concept of God trouble me?

Is it because I would have to realize I'm not really in control?
Man it seems
But not to be believed
Would I have to recognize I don't know everything?
Everything isn't good - for my good

Perhaps it's just misunderstood
All by some grand design – my enemy is not my enemy but a distant friend
My enemy – frienemy
I just have to ask, who decided that?

By some weird collection of facts or fiction
Print or diction
The devil moves about like a lion
Jesus is the Lion of the tribe of Judah
I think I would choose to be with the real.

Elevator Dreaming

I dreamed a dream that caused me to hope
Can you tell me what my dream means?
Can you tell me why my life is so?

If I were not here where would I be?
I walk the streets in search of the divine
But every door I come to is closed
And my how unfriendly these people seem to be.

I think it better I should travel on another road
But as I go a parking deck appears in my way
What is this new trial I have to face?
I enter the deck with little light for me to see
Very few cars and a strange feeling washes over me
I feel

I am being pulled to the lower level of this place
Even as I resist I seem doomed to accept my fate
But as my resistance grows the pull gives way
And thus I continue

I walk there appears a gravel slope
I examine the slope and see tire tracks where others have traveled down this path
There are also power lines that spread across
I decide there is no reward for me to go down this road
I turn back

As suddenly as I decide the road turns to a ledge
I'm on it with no place to go
I, being mildly concerned, about heights
Begin wondering why no one is taking up my cause
After being there for a time I decide

This is not the place I desire to be.

Instantaneously the ledge is lowered and I'm free to leave
As I walk along strange streets I see people I've known
Traveling a way I no longer desire to go
And I'm immediately returned to the parking deck.

But now it seems a stairwell that is barely lit
And there's an elevator and a steep flight of stairs
Personally I would prefer the elevator but for the stairs I was fully committed
I begin to climb the stairs and noticed a bright light
I awaken to find the day outside my window
The night has taken flight.

A Personal Thought:
As strange as this dream was I immediately understood what it meant.
An elevator travels both ways - fast to rise; fast to descend.
Often times against your will… you get on thinking it's going up but somebody already called it down. It makes you really pay attention.
With stairs though, even as stairs similarly aid in one's ascent and descent. Start at the bottom or the top and you will only get to where you're trying go. And there's always the opportunity to turn back.

Arise

Broken and scarred
Alone it seems, if only for a moment
Rest has entered but a name has been called
Arise.

Worried and wearied
Hurt and confused
Infused with purpose
You hear a last breath
Yet I pause to
Arise.

Gathering up what little strength
Easing out the old fate
I heard a voice
I know my name
Arise.

I am not dead.
I am not dying
I am
Becoming…
I will
Arise.

Not to new
But true life waits
Afraid before
I laid me down
And then I heard the sound - the voice say
Arise.

Get up!
Get thee up!

Richard L. Toney

Wake yourself!
Arouse the troops!
Trouble is near
I fear having soon to surrender
But my fiber - Dares you
Arise.

I am not broken
I am not scarred
I am not gone beyond despair,
Beautifully marred
I know the sound
What I must do…

Daydreaming

If you've ever dreamed a dream that plays out a movie scene
Something that you have known
Something you've nurtured

If you've ever had a dream with unrelated yet recognizable things
Something that you have seen
Something you'd pondered

If you've ever had a dream that seemed so farfetched you can't imagine what's next
Something you have heard
Something of reality

Fact is dreams consist of all these things
We've seen, we've heard, we've known
A song and a whisper turn back; make a change - it's not real
Nothing to hide from
Only a guide
There's more to life than feelings

The Morning Prayer

I wake to see the things I missed
Once ignored
Now ingrained within
I am God's son

Wavering
Disingenuous
Walking back to past discretions
God I will…
Your will be done

Correct me
Check me
Make me into the image of He
As you will…
Your will be done

Making no effort to feign sleep
I dare no longer dismiss
I've failed
Succeed with me
Bring me into this new day of life
As you will
Shine your light thru me

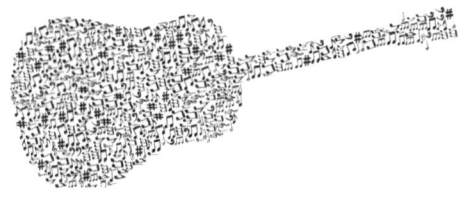

Less of a Reflection of We
03

Looking in a mirror, I can see myself – the physical me… the visible abilities of a body which at times often belies the nature of the man I believe I am. Looking strong even in its weaknesses, believing in a strength, which is as frail as the man himself. Having long ago departed when I discovered the love in my life was gone.

Even now, I fight to not accept the fact. I am just a man.

Frail and hopeless except for the hand of God. The tender grasp of a father looking in on his son as he learns the depths of his love. Given the foundation of a strong courageous mother whose measure never seemed to end even as I intently yearned for more.

An ever-wanton son slowly grasping, alone I could learn to achieve. I could learn to fail.
But by myself I would not have come here. I couldn't stand in the mirror thinking, knowing… there is a God on who I must lean.

Richard L. Toney

Unseen

Alone I stand in the eyes of man
Spectators are not privileged to the weights I bear.
Anyone who could really see
Shouldn't find it hard to believe that
As large as my load is - I don't care.
Why despair I know what I see
For what is unseen in their dreams
Is so picturesque to me, the rest stop ahead - mile marker 515.
To see me burdened – heavy-laden weighted in mind
Might cause you to miss this sign
Rest for the weary – Trading Places …exit 5-5-5.
To think all the time I traveled this highway
I never knew it was there
There's not a large building or a parking lot
No restrooms I see
Just a Rock a Tree a Beautiful Spring
And a sign that reads….Cast your Cares.
What greater relief for the burdened soul
To have a place to lighten the load
To ease my mind for the journey ahead

The latest weather forecasts a storm moving in fast
But all my baggage is gone I travel on wondering
What's next on the beaten path?
Then I think
Wasn't it odd all the people on this road
Yet the only one at the rest stop was me
Me and my load that heavy load that the spectators could see
While that beautiful sign pointing to this beautiful place
No one seemed to read

There is rest ahead

My Fathers Voice

How often I yearned to hear his voice
In my youth I cried my mother was there
In my despair I wept my brothers were there
In my necessity I worked like a slave because there was no other way
Where is my Father?

Speak to me, please
Are you there?
Do you even care I need you?

I've fallen of my bike
I've lost my keys
I need you everybody is laughing at me

Where are you?
Why don't you answer?
Don't you care? I'm perishing I'm crying
Where is my Father? Speak to me Please

Did I do something wrong?
Do I not please you?
I know I was loud. I'm Sorry!
I know I'm not like you. I'm Sorry!
I know I ask for too much. I'm Sorry!
I Promise not to do it any more

Please speak to me?
Where are you my Father?
Why don't you answer?
Do you even care?

I need you Father. I don't understand my emotions

I need you Father. I keep falling off the wagon
I need you Father. I'm scared my enemies are growing

Where are you? Answer me... Please!!!
Don't you care about me, I'm your Son.

You are my Father why won't you answer me?
I'm waiting………………..tick tock tick tock
Answer me! What did I do wrong?
Please just answer me

Then a word   {Listen}
I hear the wind   {listen}
It's raining outside   {listen}
All I here is noise: What am I listening for?
Don't you want to speak to me???
Then nothing no noise no rain no wind
What just happened?
I don't hear anything: I just went Deaf?
But then a voice:

I hear you
I have known you
I have cared for you
I gave you your mother
I gave you your voice
I gave you the wind and the rain
Each time you cried I took away your pain

I heard you……
So I whispered in the Wind
My tears were the rain to comfort you
The noise was my voice for you to know
You are always in my heart
Hear me now my son: For I have always heard you
And I will always listen to you

Things I Thought of When I wasn't Allowed to Sleep

    Hell hath no fury
But that doesn't mean the fire isn't hot
    If every time I try to sleep the phone starts to ring
Wouldn't that be an indication I need to be up doing something?
    The apple doesn't fall to far from the tree
What if I was born an orange?
    Searching for love; looking for lust
You're better off alone because John 3:16 sums it all up
    If men and women are like Mars and Venus
Why are we both on Earth? Better still who put us here
    With friends like you
Do you really need friends like me?
    If a lie gets bigger and bigger
How much bigger is the truth?
    Yesterday was today in reverse
Today is the day I break tomorrow's curse - I am now free

The Truth…

- LOVE → Lies On Virtually Everything
- HATE → Hides All The Evidence
- HOPE1 → His Opinion Possesses Errors
- HOPE2 → Her Opinion Ponders Evidence

HOPE 1&2 → the Garden of Eden…..Adam thought, Eve reasoned; both got put out for committing high treason

Gravity
    → The path of least resistance going down
    → The road less traveled going up
    It's all in how you look at it, whether you're going in the right direction.

FEAR
→ False Evidence Appearing Real
→ Faith Erases All Reservations

LIFE
→ Living In Failed Existence
→ Love Incurs Favor Exponentially

The Mind's Ear

The first voice I hear is God
God always tells me what is right
But I don't often listen

God says go right
I ask why? Raise the question and then go left
My first mind says kick a field goal
I go for the two point conversion
Life is a risk… Right?
A journey of risks versus rewards
The ultimate game of chance
Nothing ventured, nothing gained

The first thought is to avoid all trouble
The second is to deal with tolerable stress
The third says there are only two questions
So there is a 50/50 chance I'll pass this test

The first thoughts I entertain are often
The thing most in need of a change
Or things that are wrong with me

Ask yourself this question
If my first mind says there is danger to the left
Why don't I consider that in my first steps?
Why am I so afraid of going right?

The left I know
Left is the shortest distance home
Left is the cheaper gas station
Left is the way I have traveled for years
Why would I want to go right?

What is so great about going to the right?
Right is not my way home
I may go thru hell on the left
But right has a situation of its own
Knowing all this and analyzing the odds
Why would my intuition say go right?

My sixth sense says listen to my first mind
My first mind is always right
But all the roads I take in life I go left because
It's been the road that always seemed alright
But let's think for a moment
I started this journey saying God is always right
The first voice I hear is God
Intuition?   Sixth Sense?
First thought?   First Mind?
Hearts desire?
All of these things are the same
The first thought in my human brain

God Lead the way!

The Addict

O fair-weather fruit I tried
My desire is now filled
But soon I know it'll be trying.
You being such a delight
In my sadness you're a sore sight
How is it I cannot have you the way you hold me?

I am drawn to your light as the flower draws the honeybee
I am wanton for you
You are everything I think I need
I would nurture you and care for you with the fiercest joy
If only you would be a friend and stay.
Would you promise to stay with me?

O to have you with me always
I would never be afraid to walk on water for you
You wouldn't allow me to drown
Would you?

No you would have hold on me even unto death
Your sweet benign
When even my hope is gone
What I would do to have you
I wouldn't need sun or moon for you would be my night and day
You and I.

Together united
Unless you decide to depart from me
Abandon me to the lonely
You wouldn't dare would you?

Leave me to my own devices

Richard L. Toney

To my query and care
What shall I do if you go?

My Cup to Drink

Who is able to taste my pain?
Is there anyone even willing?
Is there anyone who can stand the bitterness I drink daily?
Is there no one who can stand the stench of this sorrow which
overwhelms me to the point of tears?
And yet I drink…

Is there anyone who will help me,
Who will take this cup from my hand but for a moment?
All I ask is for a brief rest; that is my earnest desire
That this jagged pill be wrenched from my stomach
So that I am never again to feel this pain
But only for a little time.

I would take this cup back without hesitation
If just for a moment I could rest
I would drink from this cup a thousand times
If for this once someone would hear the depths of my sorrow
If someone would hear my pain and drink with me
Drink for me that I might rest.

Alas I pray for that healing grace of which so many speak
But it has yet to come for me
Perhaps it is lost or I have failed to find its way.

I seek only a break to sooth this bitter drink
To quench this desire to pour more wine in this cup
Thinking death would then overtake me
Would I even if my anger were spicy enough
Love to add it to the ingredients of this my drink
Perhaps then the taste would go away
And I would be free.

Free to experience life as it is described by the artist

Natural and full of beauty
Free to experience life as it is described by the preacher
So full of hope and grace
Never having to experience this drink again
But rather living as though the cares of my youth are gone away.

I would only have that someone take this cup from my hand
My thirst would be more pleasant to me than to continue in this same drink
Knowing my intent
Knowing that there is no life for me at its end
When it is gone so am I
Gone as if I had never lived
And never known the gift of life
All because I drink.

My soul could better stand a season of drought
If knowing I would no longer have to taste this pain
I would no longer have to taste this strong drink
Death would no longer be my friend plotting my betrayal
But the one I gladly face knowing in the end there is life.

There is life if only I could pass this cup
If I could have but a brief rest so that I may see how much I have drank
How much more of this I am to endure
How long till I am free?

I ask and suddenly a hand appears who takes my cup
Drink no more he says
And I weep
Because I now know the price he has to pay
The price he pays for me
That I may be free of this drink.

The Tyranny of Man's Love

I love you so much I'm happy when I'm gone
So much so I couldn't wait to leave home
O how I love you;
You think just like me
It's a shame how many things on which we can never seem to agree
I love you so much
I would give you my entire world
Just as long as I hold the lease and you don't get on my nerves
You don't know how much love I have for you
But you will if you keep on doing what you do
O I love you

As long as I'm at the head of the table and you are next to me
But I tell you don't keep making the mistake of sitting in my seat
I love you with everything I have
I'd give you my last
But in five years with interest I expect it all back
I love you

I love you more than I ever loved my first love
Even though
Till I met you they were the worst mistake I could think of
I still love you;
So much so when you are awake I can't sleep
I lay there pondering what it is you love about me

Do you love me with a heart full of no regrets
Or is it the love of my weekly paycheck
And still I love you

O how I love you let me count the ways
But while I'm counting are you counting the days

Until I'm dead and gone hoping I leave it all to you
You say you love me but how can I really be sure
How can I know if your love for me is pure
See you don't know the amount of love I have for you
And I don't know the amount of love you have for me
But on this one thing we always seem to agree

What's yours is yours and what's mine in mine
And as long as we keep separate accounts our love will be just fine

The Truly Desperate

Imagine a scene.
Every trouble you have ever known
Knocks down your door and pushes you to the floor
And you weren't even planning on answering it.

All you can find is your phone
All the combinations you can dial nobody answers you are all alone
Wondering what price do you have to pay?

Your burdens have risen to take what you hold dear
Your life
Nine-one-one, four-one-one, one-one-two they all laughed
I am trying hard to reach an ambulance I am dialing so fast
And yet I can't even get a dial tone.

Of every combination of phone numbers I tried
I finally realize there was an operator standing by
That's what the TV said
I finally see that all it takes is one button, one man
One person waiting for me to take his hand
Jesus he's just a Prayer away.

Imagine again. Now I'm stuck in quick sand
Nobody is around nobody I can see
It's all on my shoulders I'll have to rescue myself
But I can't swim.
There's a branch to the right I lunge and grab it
But is not attached to the tree now I want to panic because I can't swim.

There is a rock to the left I'll use it as a stepping stone
But how deep is this pit and why am I out here alone

Richard L. Toney

I wonder
O how I pray someone would pick up the phone

And then I realize
All my works don't guarantee my safe return when I go out .

So the moral:
- o   When you've tried everything else; try Jesus
- o   When you've called everyone else; call Jesus
- o   When you've seen all the doctors; see Jesus
- o   When everything is wrong; Jesus is right
- o   When I can't think of it; Jesus is the answer

The Gift

Blessings abound daily from the Lord
From the air you breathe to the life you lead
You are blessed
Your sacrifice but a moment of time
To give honor to him
To thank He who has given you provisions of life
You see his reflection in your mirror
His power is the witness of your eyes
Ask yourself how many people are worse off than you
Then ponder on exactly what they do to get through
You must know you are blessed

You have been given a gift to speak
The words you choose dictate the life you lead
You have been given a gift of hands to work
The work you choose dictates the pay you receive
You have been given a gift of legs to walk
The path you take dictates the trouble you shall see
You have been given a gift of a beautiful mind to learn
The things that enter dictate the sights of your concern
I told you you're blessed

You have indeed been given a gift
How many people have the ability to live the life you live?
Whether rich as kings or poor as shepherds
Your experiences are what hold your house together
And together there is strength

Ask yourself how it would feel if I lost a gift
Would I curse the day I was born?
If everything I have known passed away
Would I still cherish seeing another day?

O blessed above the beasts of the field
Why do you not see all the gifts I have stored for thee?
It's not my question…
Yet you define yourself with the things you do not see
You want what they have but not the troubles
Definitely not the pain of waiting
And yet this is what you think of as blessed
This is what you call my gift
But what about life???

The Point Advantage

Standing at the top of the mountain
With no place to go but
Further and further till I reach my end
The race is not over

Downward I descend
To the very end I keep going
Easy is the trial difficult is the storm
Dare not sleep in the valley

Rest in a cave where it's safe
Safety
Little compromise but tough to get into
Inescapable the doubt that I've been here before
Out on a ledge

I hear my enemy out on a prowl
But I'm not worried
I'm more concerned for the days ahead
The journey
Can't stop now
Too far to travel too far gone

Only a brief opportunity to speak my peace
Carry me home
Peace and safety
Carry me home

That always seems to get me through
The daily ascent
Fight my battle
Victory on the other side

Richard L. Toney

The rough side
The further side
I scale and descend
Till when
My time comes

Standing at the foot of the mountain
Shadows everywhere
But I'm not worried or afraid

I'm
On my way home

Shake It Off

Every pain can be released
Every burden can be borne
You can be set free
All you have to be willing to do is shake it off

Foolish as it seems why not try it
Are you too proud?
It seems stupid
I might agree if it hadn't worked for me
You say really - how do I ease a broken heart?
Shake it off

Shake It Off
We have to know we are not animals
We are not like the pack mule
But for the thought realize
When the pack mule gets tired of carrying the load
What does it do?
Breakdown or
Shake it off

When a dog gets wet and doesn't want to carry the extra water
What does it do?
Shake it off
You may proudly complain that your load is too heavy
You say your burdens are too much
Shake it off

Shake It Off
When my pains are too much I shout to my father
No need for a whisper
You can as well
But first you have to lose your pride

Look foolish for a while
Shake it off

Pride kills!
Think about it – I lose my stresses
Heart attacks have to go
Ulcers have to go, colds have to go
When I shake off my burdens my body is only working on advancing my cause
Sickness can't attack if your defenses are acute and aware
So shake it off

Accept your freedom
Loose your joy
Just shake it off!
Try it
Be foolish for a moment
Ignore the pain or take a pain pill
Feel your joy be loosed
Just be willing to
Shake it Off

The Road Less Traveled

I Think:

The road less traveled is full of potholes for nobody cares for this road
It is a means to an end
The road to hell is paved with good intentions
Yet many more travel this road
With what most would call lifelong friends
Have you ever really noticed though one side is always in need of repair?
You might have also noticed one side is constantly being paved

See more specifically
A road with so many travelers must get worn out
It must get littered and displeasing to the eye
Yet so many travel it, willingly

Ask yourself why?
Or how many highways have you traveled that look similar
- always under construction
How many highways have you seen where one side is paved the other is not
It's constantly in need of repair

Take a good look at those roads and think
One reason the governments are building more highways is to move more people more easily
Because,
More people are driving more people are traveling more people are using the roadways

But it goes deeper

More people are traveling

More people are driving
More people are undertaking a journey but what is their destination?
What is yours?

The road to hell is paved with good intentions
The road to hell has a lot of travelers
The road to hell has the only government official who wants people to access and move more freely on his highway.

Constantly In Need of Repair:
This roadway
On the other side;
The road less traveled.

For as many people as ride the paved road the return trip is always full of potholes especially if you realize this isn't the way to go.
Wouldn't it be reasonable then to expect stumbling blocks, traffic delays, accidents, even slow drivers, plot-holes and unexpected twists?
Think about it the governor doesn't want you to leave his territory you can't pay his taxes if you are not there.
Satan wants you to bear his cross for him with him. Since he is guilty why shouldn't you be as well? That's why one side is paved. That's why the roadside is so carefully maintained and manicured.
Man appreciates beauty.
That is his wanton expectation, but what is true beauty when the beautiful on the surface is deceased?
While the road home is full of potholes doesn't it offer some interesting stops?

Meditate on this

If I ran out of gas, on the return home wouldn't some Good Samaritan traveling this same road stop and carry me to the gas station. Better still roadside assistance is only a call away.

Now meditate on this same spot on the paved side of the highway doesn't it always seem my phone doesn't have service in this area I'm out of range. Or nobody even thinks of stopping I have to walk five miles to the nearest station. I don't even have a gas can.
Why then is this road as beautiful as the road with potholes? The answer being; I'm familiar with it.
Nothing will make you travel more readily than knowing where you are going. But why would I go to a place I know it's going to be a hard road returning from? Why spend time on a place where…
We have the ability to choose, and as powerful a tool as this is; We're also limited to our own perspective.

This Road is Dangerous

Scenarios:
If I know there is a party to the north and a party to the south. North is closer, but I know more people going south. Which party do I go to?
Now if I know the party to the south is going to be fun and the party to the north is going to be an experience. Which party do I go to?
Now if I know the party to the north goes up a high mountain and the party to the south is in a valley which way do I go?
Now if I know I have to walk to both parties which do I go to?
Finally if I know only one person at the party to the north and everyone at the party to the south which party am I going to?

To Think:
The road less traveled gets me to a place I have never been.
The road full of potholes takes me in a direction I haven't gone before.
The party to the north is by invitation only and I got one everybody didn't.
The Government in this great city truly cares for me.
The pathway of greatest resistance is often the path to the richest reward.

Which road do I truly desire to go?

The Power in You

You who are made in the image of the Most High
You who are clothed by the Father of mercy
You who are blessed with life {strength; health; knowledge}
You who are capable to bear witness of the Power
You who can speak
Who can see;
Who can hear;
You whom was known before your birth
You who has been readied for these times
Where is your Power?

Is it buried in you?
Covered by your inability?
Covered by your iniquity?
by your past transgression?
by your Burdens?
by your education?
by your fear!!!
Loose Your Power!

The Power in you
The Power given to you
You who are made in his image

Heaven and Earth cannot bind you
For these shall pass away
But your Power
the Power in you
will be here eternally

The same Power that created you
The same Power that shapes you
The same Power that Clothes you
The Power that keeps you, you

Do you know you are powerful?

I speak to you
Your voice - silent by fear, by mellow drama
Your heart – clogged with indecision, diseased by hate and blame
Your Sight – blind by the arrogance of choice, hindered by quiet ignorance
No more.

Today you
Release the power in you

Forgive Me

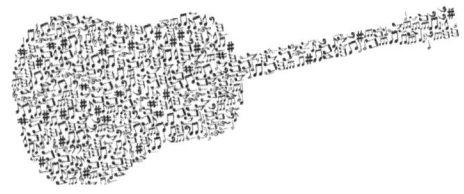

The Taste of Sour Milk
04

Imagine a grand paradise, elegant with indescribable beauty but everything around you is poison. For days and weeks, you enjoy the beauty yet there is nothing for you to eat. There is no food to sustain you and the day comes when your stomach can't take anymore. It doesn't care it wants to be fed regardless the threat of death. All the while your mind refuses, it wants no part of dying, it can't choose to sacrifice its life, and so you starve.

Too afraid of death, too weary of life, and cursed by the unknown because I should've mentioned, no one said everything around you is poison (to you).

It was only said there are poisonous things where you live… and because you refused to learn which they were now you are unsure of what to eat, and curse the man who travels with a basket of summer fruit.

Forgive Me

Fatal Rose

Charming beautiful fragrant rose
Who could know the pain you hide
Your wonderfully colored petals deceived me
I should have known there was a more painful side
I should have learned by now to ignore you from afar
But your fragrance
It draws me

As a honeybee
Into the hidden web of deceit I climb
Knowing the signs, I still blindly disregard
Never thinking it could be this bad
They say it's in my nature
I say…
Is it natural to choose not to act?

One can never be so sure after all
One can learn wrong
One can be mistaken
One can be fooled
You and the spider
Spinning a tale
Beauty and fragrance beware
Instinct or not

Be prepared for the mystery of life is
Thorns and thistles may wound your hide
But beauty is dangerous if you don't look around

Too Hungry to Eat

I'm staring at my plate
The plate before me
It's full of good things
Yet I won't eat it
I didn't fix it
I didn't ask for it to be fixed
And yet here it is before me
He brought it, the server did, to me…
Myself alone
Looking at it I sit

I can tell the chef spent much time here
The presentation is good
It pleases my eye
The smell is wonderful
Grabbing my mind – my full attention
And all around I hear how good everyone's meal is
All my senses would seem to agree
And yet I haven't had a taste

I still haven't eaten
I can't
I can't help but wonder why me?
Why now?
Why…?
…when so many are in need
Is this plate for me?

Everything looks good
They even managed to get all my favorites on the plate
And yet I still don't eat
I wonder

I search for the server
It seems he's no longer there
I'm confound
I look around
And that's when the man sitting next to me taps my shoulder
He reminds me...
I thought you were hungry - why don't you eat
Not that the food was getting cold
I look
And say to myself
I don't believe I'm worthy

This has to be a dream

The Fear

What if I fail?
If I fail having tried
Am I a failure
If so
Does that make me less than a man?
Does it make me less than?

I am not a failure
I have succeeded at trying
I am a success I think
Unless I fail giving up
Having failed at trying to give my all
Then discovering there wasn't much there to begin with
There was no use in trying
No point in being tried
Unless success was pointing out what a failure I am
Your Honor, I plea guilty.

I am guilty
Egregiously so
I wanted to win
I took shortcuts
I had to win
It cost lives, but I tried
I can say that
Although my goal was victory.

I didn't achieve it
but I learned
I am a failure
I failed
Can't I just be happy?

Richard L. Toney

Some die finding this out
This came to me with little effort
Until I realized you're dead already
Dead because you've quit fighting to live
And life was on the other side of the wall

Children

A young people lost in the desert
Hungry
Worried
Where is the life of promise?
When do we eat?

Can't go back
Forward looks barren
Walking all day
I am so tired of this heat
Where is our great promise?

So much have I given up
So far have I come
And yet happiness escapes me
Where is this new life?
This unending joy

My rations are near gone
My mule is tired
I surely didn't expect this
And yet I believed
You told me I had great hope
Where is this promise?
Where is this great for sure?

With my last breath I could curse
That is little consolation
So I walk on
Murmuring
Wondering
Why couldn't I just be happy yesterday?

Then my mule dies
Water exhausted
I must now carry the pack
My choice
Some new life
And yet they still say great promise lies ahead

I can see it - I lie
I laugh
Crying inside
Ready to curse as the scorpion nips my heal
Where is this land of the free?
This land of great promise

I stumble
Steadying myself
At my feet falls a book
Was this in my pack?
Thinking aloud - from where does this book come
A welcome distraction
I read as I walk
The sun begins to burn less

Maybe or not
Perhaps I am ignoring it more
Perhaps death has me in its grasps
And I no longer care
Perhaps I am not worthy of the promise
Why then did I leave?

I ask myself
Even as I turn the pages
Never noticing my pack has fallen off
There are the last remnants of yesterday
The times I so cherished
Reading has made me unaware
And also the murmuring has eased
I look up

Still no land of promise though

My hope freshly crushed
I go back to reading
Walking
Never noticing my belongings are gone
Until it begins to rain and then…
I stop
I look around
My pack is gone
What shall I do now?
What value to me is a promise?

Can't go back
Forward looks so desolate
Yet the ink never fades on the pages
So I continue on
Walking
Reading
Wondering where is the land I have rejoiced
Sang songs we have
Held my curses I have
And yet I see no land of the free
Are we worthy of this promise?

I am assured
Reassured
So I walk on
Pack-less
Wet
Irritable and yet engrossed in this book
Traveling on
Never noticing
The sand has become considerable soft
Almost cool
Looking down I realize
It is grass

I am no longer in the dessert
There is a spring ahead
It would seem I have reached my promise
Could this be so?

I ask aloud
I'm told to rest
I ask again
Knowing the answer is no
I now see this oasis has begun to fade
Why couldn't I be quiet?
Is rest so hard to understand?

I pick up my book
It would seem my friends have prepared me a new pack
Just as I had come to enjoy being rid of the old
I take it and begin the journey ahead
Looking back
I think
Looking forward
I see mountains ahead
I ignore the promise
Now I wonder
Where will this journey end?
At least the desert was flat

Blood and Water

Blood on my hands
Your hands

Murderers
Co-conspirators
We killed Him
Lies
Deceptions
Fornications
Sins are what they call them
That makes you and I sinners

Does it matter who is more
You more than me
I more than you
The debate never ends
Sever the trial
Both defendants guilty as hell
Guilty as charged
Like an episode of law and order
Special Victims Unit
Subtitled - Shedders of innocent blood

Why
I don't know why I did it
I don't know why you do it
It's easy to lay blame
The devil made me do it
Yet I didn't resist
Don't resist
I mean what harm could it do
How harmful can it be?
Until the gavel knocks

Guilty
Sentence
Death
No life on the other side
No more chance to say…
I'm sorry
I repent
I apologize… Forgive me?
Father, lead me not into temptation

Low Rent Construction

A house that's half built won't shelter you from the rain.
How is it then you want to do half the work, but expect the full days pay?
What is the source of this original logic?
The deception: The lie that we deserve life
How can we deserve life when we fail to recognize the great light?
When you build a house you begin with a foundation

Who is yours?
After the foundation the outer walls are erected
Who put them together?
After that the roof is added
All these things before you begin putting siding in its place
Where did this blueprint come from?

Is it DNA?
Is it science,
Some great race from the unknown heavens?

Ask yourself then
Is it so bad to be torn down?

If a house is not built on a sure foundation
Wouldn't reconstruction be desired?
Don't lie…
You would love it if your current house were renovated at no cost to you?

Why not then accept the gifts from the ultimate contractor?
God's Construction Company designs by the designer

When God builds does he not build perfectly?

Richard L. Toney

Everything working together
For they that love the Lord

So why not accept his service
Exchange your used and contrived heart for a pure new one
Surrender your battered and worn spirit for a new spirit of joy
Release your ragged and torn flesh for a new indestructible body
All these things provided at no cost to you
Little Costs
The cost of letting go

Hunger Pains

A feast is prepared
But lest I perish
I dare not eat
I'm not sure this is for me.

How am I to know if the master desires my hand to eat from his table?

My people are lowly farmers
Heavy laborers
Fit for clean-up work at His stables
How dare I be so bold as to take and eat?

Even though the table is set with such treats
I sit and I wonder
Why has the master called me into his house?
I pray I have not offended him.
Having failed yet again to be devout
Is it because I'm in trouble
Is that why He invited me?

Surely my master must know I wouldn't be here otherwise
Yet here I stand
Waiting his arrival with anticipation and fear
O how I would love to taste the fruits of his table
In my lust I hurry his arrival to quail this temptation
I am not strong enough to resist

I would not dare offend the master by taking from his feast
But my heart does cry
And my stomach does ache to taste such exotic meats

I would labor more into the night for just a morsel of what is prepared here
Yet since I haven't been told I just stand back in fear
Waiting

And then upon my Master's voice I begin to plead
King
My stomach speaks a ravenous need
Mighty King I do not dare take of your table
I would only ask a small portion of meat

Yet my stomach has betrayed me
Grumbling

O sovereign king I pray that you would not send me away
But yet allow me to wash thy feet to appease my disgrace
He doesn't speak

And then to my surprise my king takes hold of my hand
And says
For you my servant I have commanded this feast
All that is prepared is for you to take and eat
You may go until your stomach is filled bursting with joy
Take your measure and be filled this today is your day
You are servant no more
You are free

Little Mountain Pass

How hard is it to pedal up a hill?
Ask any child they say it's impossible for her or him
But how hard is it for you?

You say but a mere thought
And then you realize the mountain you have wrought
It wasn't there before
Yet here it is
This too shall pass

The smallest hill is like a mountain to a young rider
But you are experienced
A devout mountain climber
Yet you tremble at the thought of traveling this hill
Turning back
This too shall pass

The pains it would cause if you were to fall
Even worse if you were not able to reach the top
Fear swelling
Rage inside
Why is it this mountain I've chosen to climb?
You ask yourself
Is this too big?
Can I overcome this?
Here it starts.

Optimistic
And yet questioning
How is it I am on this path?
Why was there no detour to warn me of these facts?
This mountain is too steep
To ragged to be climbed

Yet there are tracks
They lead to the foot of the mountain

How odd it would seem
Someone walking this path
Even more strange
There is no trail going back
The more I examine it
The more I fell
This too shall pass

Discouraged or disquieted
I think it better I should turn away
Certainly this is not the path a rider should take
How could I even dream of pedaling up this pass?
Such ragged edges and not a single blade of grass
In case I fall
And there's no one else around

I would lay injured lost amongst the rocks and trees
Battered and broken
All alone to succumb to my fate
Surely this is a mistake
Not the end befitting of me
Lost and alone, in such a desolate place;
Trying to climb a mountain with no ending or peak
I've chosen to head on this path

Onward
Upward
How funny it seems
There are footprints in the dirt the same as me
Strange because I've never seen this place before

I climb
I pause
I rise
I fall

Forgive Me

Missing the sign that says
Leave your baggage below

Richard L. Toney

A Song of Adoration

My Father – I call you Father
For me there is no other
Holy beyond what I know
Powerful is thy grasp
Never are thy children far from thee.

Thy sweet majestic name reigns higher than all
My God
My King
Today I call you
Jehovah.

Fill me with thy breadth of life
Make me know as I am known - as you are
Bread of life
Angel's food
Fulfilled in Your Son
I ask but a taste.

May be more than I could handle
But you know best
My Lord
My Provision
Jehovah
Jireh.

A name
A revelation
I seek the living water
Make it rain on me according to the portion I have believed.

I bid thee Father
Master
Savior

The Climb

What is it to overcome?
At what point does one start?
And better, is there an end to the drama?
People say all the time they overcame
The odds
The struggle
What do they really know about me?
My pain
My storm swept seas?

Have you ever been hurt by the mere sounds of life?
Do you have insufferable kids?
A nagging wife?
A boss who doesn't here the you who speaks?
What is it then you can say about overcoming

I've seen the bright side
It's even more of a struggle to get through than the storm
And yet you ask me go for it
Look past that which burdens me
Look past the troubles
Look past
To the hills which cometh…
Storms

Chaos
I no longer search for shelter
I say, bring it on
Bring it all to the surface to be seen
All to the surface to be clean and known
And then maybe I too will overcome
Or be swept away
Finished

Richard L. Toney

No more hiding
No more pain
No more fear
Know more me
Know more Him
It has been revealed
He said you will make it to the other side

A Prayer of Faith

Father give ear to my words
I acknowledge my faults
I offer my failures to you as a gift
For you to use as you see fit

This broken vessel
This tattered rag
Only you can make me what I am - supposed to be
Only you can make me worthy
So I ask you now

Hear my heart
It cries for thy forgiveness
It yearns to be near you
I have little to offer that is not already yours but
My sacrifice of faith
I offer my body

All that is within me
Everything I touch
Use it for your glory
Use it for your honor
Use it to its best ability to glorify heaven

You know best what is best

My strength
My character
The volume of me
Be tested - approved
And made complete in you

Beyond the image

May I receive the promise,
A place in your kingdom
A room in the house of your dear Son
In whose name I speak
Thank You
    Jesus

Forgive Me

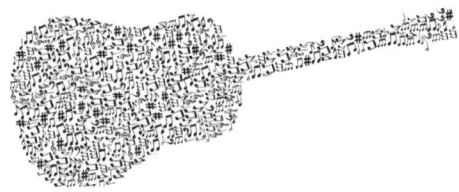

Dear Brother - No More Am I Afraid 05

The world may not understand me or my message but who am I to judge if you are right or wrong?

This odyssey focuses on you and me. Intelligence and understanding, while both are good food, neither make one complete. Studying on who I am in Christ, again good measure, but what about my brother?
Even those who don't believe in God are conditioned to love. We are bound by love and to love. Love is the first commandment and it is the essence of our humanity. Why then is there racism, hatred and war?

The simplest answer is -we have forgotten how to love. The larger truth being we are afraid to, love, because love as we have learned it is impure and often hurtful.

Think about it love implies a commitment to excellence, which means if I see you failing I help you succeed and you don't get upset and discouraged you get delighted.

It is said you can't have love without hate. What about God?

God loved us so much he gave himself for our shortcomings, He the Creator...

In truth _pure love_ doesn't require hate, it doesn't invite hate. It accepts hates existence and works to change it.

One thing to recognize from this reading is we are designed to love and from love. However often our learned circumstances make us choose to hate in defense to our learned imperfect love.

The Cure

I lost a finger while slitting your throat
You lay dying
I stand bleeding
The pool encompassing us both
But I never knew

I didn't feel a thing
but you having to die
I had to end you
Life as we knew it has passed
But where are the sirens

Surely someone heard the curdling screams
The anger
The colossal fight
This house is a wreck
Yet no one comes

The neighbors ignore
The passer by waves with disdain
Who cares if we both lay dead
Dying
Except I'm not
I own this moment
You are defeated
And it only cost me a finger
A little measure of blood
To assure
There will be no more offense in me

The End of Vanity

Vanity stands alone atop the cliff
Looking down
Wondering
Thinking
How does it come to this?
Is this my end?

Studied much
Learned little
Knowing it all
And yet my arrival is a mystery.

Could I be so blind?
How does it come to this?
In vain is it asked?
In vain no response
Life is what you make of it
Vanity stands perched on the edge alone

I can do all things…
Is there any more
Anything I need I can do it
My possibilities are only bound by death
As I live
I can do it alone
Vanity has stated its case
And yet on the ledge he stands alone

Looking up I see
What was never in the mirror
Clearly his time has come
Old and worn
Bitter and defeated

Afraid and without hope
Eerily he looks down
I look up
We have the same eye
And yet he is still perched atop alone

Leaning
Almost carried by the wind
Am I mistaken?
Is there suddenly fear now
Some new doubt
In despair I turn away
Wondering
How does it come to this?

Is this my end?
Has fate shown me what I have always known?
Pride will get you killed
Death comes for all
And yet the vain seem to disappear more soon
More violently.

There are ridges on the way down
Barbs
Even below there is a thicket of thorns
Yet this day he has decided to quit
He has decided alone
Almost surrendering to the breeze
And then a hand reaches out

Taking him
Pulling him back in…

Brother don't leave me

An Impasse

How can I love my brother
When he hates my God?
His words screaming he hates me
Clearly he must
His soul in need of like salvation
I would change his ways
Yet I can't talk to him

He won't learn
I won't listen
We go our separate ways
I can't believe
He doesn't believe
And yet I know - God is truth

God is God
Creator
Enabler
Designer and builder
The life of man
God though he has many names
Is the same
God for me
God to you

GOD
You might be wrong
I might be right
We say it to one another
And yet we're the same
Men
Strong
Subservient

Richard L. Toney

Different faith
Evangelical to a fault
In the end there can be only one
Though neither of us will concede who wins

Time will reveal

The Weight of the World

Responsibility's a heavy burden
Heavier than the truth
Heavier than the largest stone
So unnaturally heavy and often accident prone
No wonder we all fall down

Yet it's only the luggage of this world
Responsibility!
The one thing we all have to carry
To care for
What is my responsibility?

Truth!
The preservation and cultivation of the whole truth
Love!
The teaching and manifestations of pure unrequited love
What a heavy weight we carry
Not so heavy if that's the only thing that burdens us.

I ask myself
Why then does man suffer as we do?
Could it be
We're overburden
Packed as the common mule
The proverbial workhorse
We are not made to carry such a load that is not our responsibility
And yet we try.

Suffering into death
Saying…
Our pains and their logic is what define us
And still I can only hear it read…

Richard L. Toney

My burden is easy
My yoke is light

Father, may I rest my back

Broken Bread

A campfire by the sea is a fitting scene
I sit here alone with only a loaf of bread to eat
Bread and water and me

Bread
A symbol of strong peace
Heavy labor
And yet soft yield
The celebration of the bond between my brother and me

How we make treaties over this broken bread
We take suppence to remember our dead
We share this loaf to fulfill a promise to one another
To our mother
That regardless the storm
We will always be
Brothers

Strength and pride
A force to be seen
And yet today I sit alone
Only the sea to comfort me
The sand and tide to hide my feet
Would I cry to have him break bread with me?
Dear Father

Would I joy to share this promise?
With him
With you
Could I enjoy this loaf my bountiful feast
The wind massages
I am still alone

The beauty of this moment uninterrupted by questions
I alone share the feast with my soul
I alone surrender to the sounds of the tide
What a wonderful place to be
The more wonderful day for a feast
For my brother to partake this loaf with me
The two of us together to meet
There can be peace

Conversations With Kin

A wind is blowing
Picking up a definite fright
It's time for another summer storm
Time to clean away the stench of yesterday
The day you forgot
The day I put away
Wasted
Doing nothing of purpose.
Some call it enjoying life
And yet wish for more as dawn approaches
Hoping night doesn't beckon them home
The end is near
Nearer
Nearing
What can I do?

Knowing the end
I can't change
Knowing the beginning
I can't change
Knowing there is labor in between
What does my work mean?
Should I labor in vain?
What do I do?

What can I do to change?
You
Me
The living we do
The life, which is void
Devoid
Missing meaning
And yet meaning is there

Losing purpose
When all along purpose is there
There is some value
Will you work with me?

We have a choice to make
I have a choice
It affects you
You have a choice
It affects me
We need each other to not take a fall
But both be damned
What can I do?

You ask
I ask
The work never getting done
As another dawn approaches
Nighttime is coming
The hour when no man can work
And yet all will be hungry
Will there be food to eat?
How can there be
There is no barn built for us

With Respect to Woman

Can you ever understand what my life demands?
Can you alone teach me to be a better man?
I feel my brothers can

I am free to rejoice with my brothers
My brothers can rejoice openly with me
Together we build a tighter family
We are the keepers of the gate

Because only my brothers know my pain
Only my brothers know the experiences I can't explain
My brothers, sometimes closer to me than my Mother
With the wisdom of ages I have yet to discover
They created my history

My brothers who have seen the path
Who offer guidance on the traps
I know of no other like my brothers
Who have seen my turmoil and know my struggle.

I don't make believe there is a special comfort like that of my mother
But the solace of my brothers
We watch each other's back

They've seen my storms and they have tasted the rains
They've experienced the winter aggravation
But still return to harvest the summer grains
My brothers teach me to plow the fields

They teach me to sow the seeds
My brothers teach me to be a mighty man of deeds
Principled

Disciplined
My brothers' keeper

My brothers teach me the thrill of the hunt
My brothers show me the joy of my praise
My brothers show me as serious as life is
The battle is already won
All there is left for me is to experience the journey
And who better to share this with than those who stand with me
My Brothers

Sword to sword we stand ready to meet every challenge
Empowering one another
Our lives in God's hand
I ask
Will you then wait for me till I get home?

Remembering Loves

Five loves have I had in my life
Yet it is said you can only love once
Perhaps then I have died four times
Reborn
Reincarnated
Revised
Re-envisioned
With no back story
Though I remember everything I lost
Everyone I used to have
They're no longer there
Here
Physically
They are with me forever as I am
Random thoughts
Unavailable
Unattached

I need my grandmother's wisdom
She would know why I feel lost
I need my father's answers
He could tell me everything I missed
I need my brother's strength
Sometimes it's hard carrying life alone
Mostly I miss my innocence
I need my innocence

Would I love anyone more?
Than to never know men can hurt you
Life has its own justification
We may never know the ends
And still
Innocently we may go along

Richard L. Toney

Picking up pebbles
Discarding stones
Ever collecting souvenirs
Until we discover
The world is full of hurts
We have become heavy with worthlessness
And here at the point of end
There is nowhere to offload the burden
Without killing the innocence of others
My grandfather would know what to do here
Alas he is gone from me as well
Too early to reveal the mystery to me
Memories are forever

A Song of Beauty

What is beautiful?
Full of beauty
Nature

Harmonious
Symbiotic
Undisturbed by greedy man
Living and living
Death is just a beginning
A transformation into something more
Something less
A memory perhaps
Like
The sun burned hotter yesterday

And still
Flowers bloomed
Seedlings became trees
Man returned to dust
Leaving behind his memories
His experiences
Relayed to another generation
Through another crop
Was he seed
Seedling
Fruit
Or sower
Some melody of all
The image of God
Beautiful
Full of beauty

At one with nature

When he fully matured
Although too many die young
Here for only a moment
Revealing promise
Then falling aside
Undignified
Like a frail blossom
Cast by the wind into the sea
Then dashed upon the rocky shore
He grew up too fast
Never fully maturing
Never taking root
Never understanding
The need for the tree
And still he was beautiful
Full of beauty

Singing his own song
His own melody
Passing it to others
Then returning to his first
The dust
Sad song
Shortened song
Unfinished melody
Still so beautiful
Full of beauty

The Exit Psalm
06

The world today revolves around relationships. Who you know, how you know them, what they can accomplish for you… it's the easiest path to achieving some measure of success. As such I present to you a relationship. Not a religion or a sect, fundamentally - a connection to more. The who or what, decided by you. Based only on what you choose to believe of my nature or me. A nature, which I learned just as you, *survival of the fittest*.

I must say though, in this journey called life we are always in varying stages of fitness. Physically fit, mentally fit, sometimes spiritually fit, yet we really never seem completely together. As you read earlier I came to recognize one important fact. We all are failures. The entire human race has failed at living.

You may ask how has man failed, yet for me the more important question is why. The answer to both questions being the same, we still don't understand life. We argue over when life begins and how life should end as if we are creators of life. The truth is before man there was life. After man there is life. We are only a part of living… a relative, as an uncle or brother. We are given a place and time to deliver and even higher, a choice in deliverance as part of the gift of life, but not the complete plan. Why you might ask? Because of our tendency to fail. Failing by choices based on what we know and whom we learn from… where our relationships lie. It seems so simple and yet, is there denying everybody knows somebody?

One thing I offer in these words is we are not designed for the life we experience. It's our learning that has made us accept it as life. But when our time comes we still must be prepared for the truth to be revealed.

The Origin

I think of him every moment I'm here
How I have failed him
I always fail him
Yet he hasn't ceased my being.

Perhaps he sees something of value in me
Something that could one day be good
A lifetime of experience for that one moment
The moment to fulfill my destiny.

To me an unbalanced trade
And yet I'm infinitely grateful for this chance
The chance to do good
To please him
My creator.

He is all I've ever known
For me he is Father
My Father
Even as I am dishonorable son.

I try though
With some sense of urgency
With some sense of hopelessness
I go on believing
Knowing there is a tomorrow.

Brighter for some
Darker to others
Assured though before the fall
At the dawn where all bear witness
All have known
Man is nothing on his own.

Of Plain Existence

Would I presume to know what is greater than I?
Can I presume to speak for he, whose voice is much stronger than mine?
I am but a man
Limited by me
Limited by him
Limited to and as an image
And yet I have his voice

The voice of my father
With clarity I see
With strength I speak
Without denial I understand
I am but a man
Weak and dependent
Flinching and unsturdy

Can I be trusted to speak truth?
Can I adequately relate love?
Love unlimited
Even as I am so short
Filled with faults
Shortcomings debuting every hour
I am just a man

His son
His servant
Some guy who loves
Believes
In love
Believes
In life
Believes

Someday there is a reward

It is just
There is no bias
No lie
No hope other than to trust
Knowing
I have earned whatever I have received

If it's bad
May someday I be made worthy of mercy

The Wailing Mirror

My heart wrenches
I tear at the clothing of my skin
Expending my life beating on a wall
Beating my head against a rock imagining I can stop this pain
Please storm be still

You see me
You see I'm at peace
You see me at ease with life
Performing a humble visage
You smell a perfume of my simulated joy
You hear my falsetto
But you don't know me
Quiet rage be hushed

Supposing we're in this together
Yet when it's time to fight you disappear
I faint away
When it's time to rejoice you beam unashamed
Yet I stand at the wall alone
Too weak to save face
But I must contend for you to ensure life
Hardened anger be quiet
Be still storm

My heart aches
Your head hurts
We are one in struggle but I bear the pain alone
Silently I scream
Quiet rage be still
Storming winds cease
There will be peace when I rise

The Wailer

There is a crier inside
Tears flooding the veins that map the man
Washing away the dirt of arrogance
The trash of deceit
The trail of failed dreams of righteousness
In his wake is a river of pain
As the lips quiver
Forgive me Lord I have sinned

The heart no longer able to contain the truth
No longer able to well the hurt
The man has chosen his lusts again
Ignoring the light within
He has chosen to wallow in darkness
Quenching the fire inside
Causing the crier to speak
Forgive us Lord we have sinned

A powerful confession
A more able cleanser than his tears alone
The break allowing the fire a breath of air
Calming the crier
Enlarging the man
Providing hope sin will soon fall away

Beyond the Friendly Confines of Adoration

A friend can be defined in so many ways
In this life, though some say there can be no friends
Real or imagined…
There are those we trust
There are those we need
There are those relative to us
There are people living and dying for and because
Calling most of them friends
Can we say…
We adore them all and most think highly of us

Knowing you well, can I call you my friend?
A friend like he who leads me safely through my lies
Thru the forest of bones of those that have died when I turned away.
A friend who shelters me from the storm of my secret frailties
Never judging me unfit for life
Declaring me worthy to be called friend.
Beyond associate companion or momentary acquaintance
Knowing only a name and some minor details
Knowing me well, can you say the same calling me friend?

A friend like him who kept you around when others tried to send you to the void
Declaring you a failure, they desired yet he never tired - discarding your life
Speaking estimable deeds of you when you were hidden by distasteful choices.

Beyond a momentary comrade, ally or distant buddy
He called you worthy - colleague,
Knowing the frailty of the hand you held of his hem
After all these thoughts I'm compelled to ask

Are we honestly friends?

Trust waning with distance
Dependence falling with each failure perceived
You may be my brother but your heart is far from me
I no longer see a love for you
Yet of you I believed
We were friends
Perhaps someday we might be again

Remembering Jehosophat

I will take my shoes and walk the distance to my home
Beginning and ending with the sea
Over the water
Thru the land
I will travel
80 years
80 days
I must go
Remembering Jehosophat

Never minding the assembly of clouds
My resolve remains
To walk the distance to my home
Can I make it alone?
I wonder
Will there be trouble along the way
I ask in prayer
The answer…
Remember Jehosophat

God is with you
His every word holding you
Take your shoes - leave doubters behind
Death awaiting the slowfully arrogant
Passing lies
Corrupting hope
Your journey is yours
Walk your way however long it takes
There is a promise of the end
Just remember Jehosophat

With one way to go
Mind your remembrance

There are ones who desire you to fail.
One who desire for you not to reach
And so your desire must be to endure
It is not such a long journey home anyway
Over the water
Thru the land
Ignoring the weather
There is always a prayer
Remember Jehosophat

God is with you

Beyond

Is there any other so bold as to say
I was there at the beginning
Certifying all things begin
As all things end
Linear
Yet not bound to or by a straight line

You see the seed
You see the tree
Yet you don't see everything in between or after
But you certify they exist
You allege to know the how
Discarding the why
Not knowing
Not seeking
It is irrelevant to you
Though you are the first to try a belief
My belief
There is a why written

A full testament
Yet incomplete
Inconceivable to an imperfect creation
Yet sufficient enough to fuel the hunger for more
There is more
Deeply rooted as the tree always bearing fruit
Even though none witnessed the planted seed
Yet all eat freely
Never saying thank you
Always seeking the moment
But disregarding why
The why being too simple to be true
Too difficult to understand how

Richard L. Toney

The answer is His love

The Passage

With every breath I take
I die a little more
Slowly returning to the state I was before
The picture from which I was created fading into a memory
With every blink I see less and less
Life going on
Passing away before my eyes
Knowing one day I too shall die
Making my story here complete

But what of my time spent, what shall be said?
Have I represented the light?
Been a spark in the dark
Am I my brother's keeper?
Truly my father's child
It's within, yet beyond me to determine
My only course is hope

So with hope I worry less
Striving more to be like the image
Accepting that I may fail
Yet I will not be a failure
I will be content

Maturity

I was born afraid
Of my youthful arrogance
Of illicit tendencies
From what I hear there's many things that I should fear
None of which is life.
I would live,
Unabashed
Unashamed
Unafraid
I, who have been blessed with this gift.
So many call it living in freedom
I call it my experience.
With youthful exuberance I pursue each passion
Wonderfully
Unafraid
Unaware, that this, as they say, would hinder my latter years.
It seems this they should have told me first
Or perhaps they did
Perhaps in my arrogance I failed to listen
I could not hear
Older and wiser
The vanity of youth being long since departed
What I would see
It proved to be beyond my time,
The view always changes.

Awakening

Looking at my watch
Seconds become hours
Hours turning to days
Days becoming years I've wasted
Hearing a melody
Revelry
The king is return
How do I in the kingdom stand?

Breaking the silence in the night air
I hear the trumpet
The hour has arrived
11:59
Many are surprised
Some have been preparing
This day, this night
Yesterday and tomorrow are changed for all
But how do I in the kingdom stand?

Sleeping long hours
Abandoning work to play
I hear Taps and yet am not compelled to move
The tune has become monotonous
The promise of little concern
Until I hear a new cadence nearing
The beating of hooves bearing a chariot
The striking of boots
His army has arrived
How do I in the kingdom stand?

Somewhat shaken
Knowing and yet ignoring
Procrastinating to the end

Richard L. Toney

I maintain no illusion of reward
I only ask to be spared
Your highness,
The kingdom and I still survive

To My Father In Heaven

I'm not certain of the truth
About you
About me
I only know I am.

From what I'm told I was born
Someday I will die
Death being a beginning or an ending
My knowledge will transform
Transfer to another time
Some other place I've never known consciously
I will no longer be me as I know
So I ask.

Make me your image
Teach me to conform to what I think is mine
Reveal to me the meaning of true love
Show me there is light beyond my dark
There is hope for me

Broken
Illiterate
Insufficient
Dying
Crying
Unworthy of you
Can I know love?

Can I know your proven passion?

The author / publisher thanks you for sharing your time with this book. We invite you to experience some other fine publications available from Life in Print Publishing.

Using the power of confession, these daily meditations are a spark to break free of secret pasts and guilt turned shame.

Turn what caused you to lose sight of being into the faith to conquer it all.

Available at Amazon and other fine retailers

You may also enjoy more voices of our published authors at: www.lifeinprint.org with more from Author R.L. Toney at www.thelionswell.com

Also available from Life in Print Publishing. Check out...

Wake your faith up!

Shake up the complacency of wanting to and be what he called you to be. Less than a moment a day for the next 14 days, feed the desire and sow a bountiful harvest toward your faith. Record your journey each day and find yourself empowered to do all He said you can do.

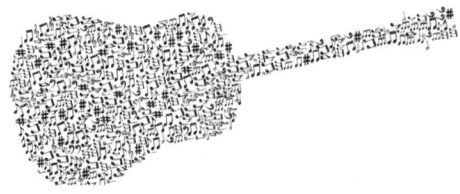

A Simple Inference

To My God,
 I Thank You for allowing me the vision to produce in my life
The strength to follow the vision
The courage to build this object for others to witness
To know, even amongst the critical thought,
All there is to see in this life.

www.ingramcontent.com/pod-product-compliance
Lightning Source LLC
Chambersburg PA
CBHW051801040426
42446CB00007B/466